IF STONES COULD SPEAK

UNLOCKING THE SECRETS OF STONEHENGE

IF STONES COULD SPEAK

UNLOCKING THE SECRETS OF STONEHENGE

by Marc Aronson with the generous cooperation
of Mike Parker Pearson and the Riverside Project

NATIONAL GEOGRAPHIC
WASHINGTON, D.C.

To Mike and the Riverside Team, my gracious hosts, guides, and advisors, and to Aiden and Ethan Pidgeon for reading the proofs and helping me to see the book with my readers' eyes.

A Book by Aronson & Glenn LLC
Produced by Marc Aronson and John W. Glenn
Book design, art direction, and production by Jon Glick, mouse + tiger
Copyediting by Sharon Brinkman

Published by the National Geographic Society
John M. Fahey, Jr., *President and Chief Executive Officer*
Gilbert M. Grosvenor, *Chairman of the Board*
Tim T. Kelly, President, *Global Media Group*
John Q. Griffin, *Executive Vice President; President, Publishing*
Nina D. Hoffman, *Executive Vice President; President, Book Publishing Group*
Melina Gerosa Bellows, *Executive Vice President, Children's Publishing*

Prepared by the Book Division
Nancy Laties Feresten, *Vice President, Editor in Chief, Children's Books*
Jonathan Halling, *Design Director, Children's Publishing*
Jennifer Emmett, *Executive Editor, Children's Books*
Carl Mehler, *Director of Maps*
R. Gary Colbert, *Production Director*
Jennifer A. Thornton, *Managing Editor*

Staff for This Book
Jennifer Emmett, *Project Editor*
Eva Absher, *Art Director*
Lori Renda, *Illustrations Editor*
Grace Hill, *Associate Managing Editor*
Lewis R. Bassford, *Production Manager*
Susan Borke, *Legal and Business Affairs*

Manufacturing and Quality Management
Christopher A. Liedel, *Chief Financial Officer*
Phillip L. Schlosser, *Vice President*
Chris Brown, *Technical Director*
Nicole Elliott, *Manager*
Rachel Faulise, *Manager*

Photography and Illustrations Credits
Abbreviations: t=top, b=bottom, l=left, r=right

Front cover: photo illustration by Toby Kroner Photography; back cover: Ken Geiger/NationalGeographicStock.com

Page 2: Ken Geiger/NationalGeographicStock.com; page 6: © All Rights Reserved. The British Library Board (Add. 28330, f. 36); page 8: from William Stukeley, *Stonehenge*, 1740, public domain; page 9: © All Rights Reserved. The British Library Board (licence number: AROGLE01); page 10: Kazuhiko Sano/NationalGeographicStock.com; page 12: National Monuments Records Center/English Heritage; pages 13 and 14 (t, br): © Aerial-Cam/SRP 2006/7/8; page 14: English Heritage; page 15 (inset): British Geological Survey/NationalGeographicStock.com; page 15 (b): Andrew Henderson/NationalGeographicStock.com; page 15 (r): NGM Maps; page 16: Andrew Henderson/NationalGeographicStock.com; pages 17–20 (all): courtesy Mike Parker Pearson; page 21: Martin Walz; pages 22–23 (all): courtesy Mike Parker Pearson; page 24: Ken Geiger/NationalGeographicStock.com; page 26: © All Rights Reserved. The British Library Board (licence number: AROGLE01); page 27 (all): courtesy Mike Parker Pearson; pages 28–29 (all): © Aerial-Cam/SRP 2006/7/8; page 30: English Heritage; page 32: English Heritage; page 33 (t): © Aerial-Cam/SRP 2006/7/8; page 33 (b): Ken Geiger/NationalGeographicStock.com; page 35: courtesy Mike Parker Pearson; page 36: © Aerial-Cam/SRP 2006/7/8; page 38: Kazuhiko Sano/NationalGeographicStock.com; pages 39–41 (all): Andrew Henderson/NationalGeographicStock.com; page 42: English Heritage; page 44: © Aerial-Cam/SRP 2006/7/8; page 45: Ken Geiger/NationalGeographicStock.com; pages 46–47 (all): © Aerial-Cam/SRP 2006/7/8; page 48: Andrew Henderson/NationalGeographicStock.com; page 50: © Aerial-Cam/SRP 2006/7/8; page 51: Andrew Henderson/NationalGeographicStock.com; page 53: © Aerial-Cam/SRP 2006/7/8; page 55: Ken Geiger/NationalGeographicStock.com; pages 56–57 (all): © Aerial-Cam/SRP 2006/7/8

The National Geographic Society is one of the world's largest nonprofit scientific and educational organizations. Founded in 1888 to "increase and diffuse geographic knowledge," the Society works to inspire people to care about the planet. It reaches more than 325 million people worldwide each month through its official journal, *National Geographic,* and other magazines; National Geographic Channel; television documentaries; music; radio; films; books; DVDs; maps; exhibitions; school publishing programs; interactive media; and merchandise. National Geographic has funded more than 9,000 scientific research, conservation and exploration projects and supports an education program combating geographic illiteracy. For more information, visit nationalgeographic.com.

For more information, please call 1-800-NGS LINE (647-5463) or write to the following address:
National Geographic Society
1145 17th Street N.W.
Washington, D.C. 20036-4688 U.S.A.

Visit us online at www.nationalgeographic.com/books

For librarians and teachers: www.ngchildrensbooks.org

More for kids from National Geographic: kids.nationalgeographic.com

For information about special discounts for bulk purchases, please contact National Geographic Books Special Sales: ngspecsales@ngs.org

For rights or permissions inquiries, please contact National Geographic Books Subsidiary Rights: ngbookrights@ngs.org

Library of Congress Cataloging-in-Publication Data

Aronson, Marc.
 If stones could speak : unlocking the secrets of Stonehenge / by Marc Aronson ; with Mike Parker Pearson and the Riverside Project.
    p. cm.
 Includes bibliographical references and index.
 ISBN 978-1-4263-0599-3 (hardcover : alk. paper) -- ISBN 978-1-4263-0600-6 (library binding : alk. paper)
1. Stonehenge (England)--Juvenile literature. 2. Wiltshire (England)--Antiquities--Juvenile literature. 3. Megalithic monuments--England--Wiltshire--Juvenile literature. I. Parker Pearson, Michael, 1957- II. Stonehenge Riverside Project (England) III. National Geographic Society (U.S.) IV. Title.
 DA142.A74 2010
 936.2'319--dc22
                                    2009028870
Printed in China

09/RRDS/1

CONTENTS

niet. Maer ghelyc het dese Saxenaers (die al heydenen
waeren) daer goed bonder hebben zy gepoocht daer te
blyuen, ende tot dien eynde soo begheerden zy met den
Conyngh Votigerno te handelen. Dwelc hen toeghelaten was.
Want den Conyngh gheen erch dynckende quam ter ghestelder
plaetse (te weten by Saltsbury) verselschapt synde met
omtrent iiij.C. LXXX van syne edelen. Maer de Saxenaers
hebbende hen seluen voorsien met wapenen ende gheweer dwelc
zy onder hun mantelen droeghen, versloeghen alle dese
Britanen ende naemen den Conyngh ghevanghen. Aurelius
Ambrosius die naer Votigerno Conyngh werdt, willende de
versleghen Britaensche edelen een eeuwyghe ghedynckenisse
oprechten, dede door de behendicheyt van Merlyn eenen
grooten hoop steenen rommen uit Irland, ende dede die
stellen op S. Ambrosius berch, die se noch staen in deser
voeghe, soo ick se selue ter plaetse uet gheteekent
hebbe.

CHAPTER ONE

THE SECRET OF STONEHENGE

STONEHENGE, NEAR SALISBURY, ENGLAND. It is a typical September day in western England—we had heavy rain yesterday, and the sky is still slate gray, but when the clouds break there are sudden moments of clear sunlight. I keep noticing the changing light because I am dashing to stay out of the way of a Japanese film crew. They are following the archaeologist Mike Parker Pearson as he leads them around Stonehenge—the mysterious circle of stones that was built on Salisbury Plain 4,500 years ago and is now a World Heritage site *(see map on pages 10-11)*.

Somebody went to great effort very long ago to shape these stones and then lift them into place. But unlike the Egyptians who were raising their great pyramids at the exact same time, the builders did not know how to write. All they left behind was this beautiful circle of stone. And so we walk around it, snapping photos, and wonder, What are you telling us, stones? What did you mean to those who put you here? We want the stones to speak. We sense that if we could only understand them, we would be able to reach back in time. We would be in the world of ancient Britain.

Lucas de Heere sketched this picture of Stonehenge (OPPOSITE) in the 1570s. The ditch and mound around the edge of the circle are still there. In fact, a bank like this with a ditch next to it is what archaeologists call a "henge." But the name Stonehenge probably has a different root: the Old English words for "stone" and "hanging"—possibly because the stones seem to "hang" in the air.

I am thrilled that Mike and the Riverside Project team are letting me tag along with them. When I was in middle school, I stayed up nights reading about the great archaeologists of the past: Heinrich Schliemann and his quest to find the real Troy; Hiram Bingham who climbed through the Andes in search of the lost city of the Incas. I loved reading about those adventures. But I also felt shut out. Everything important, it seemed, had already been found. But that

This illustration was published in 1740 by William Stukeley, one of the first to make a careful study of the grounds of Stonehenge. Stukeley believed that Stonehenge was a Druid temple, and here he imagines what an ancient Druid might have looked like.

was not true—and Mike's work right here at Stonehenge is the proof. There are still many mysteries of the past that only now—only just now—can be solved. As I discovered, when we think in new ways, the past reveals fresh secrets.

For the past thousand years, visitors have left records of what they thought the stones were saying. Stonehenge was built by Merlin's magic, or it was a Roman temple, or a Druid holy place—over and over, what people have said about Stonehenge has reflected their own beliefs and fantasies. The stones stay silent, while we view them with new eyes. Indeed, each time a new technology has been invented in the past hundred years, we have seen the entire landscape around Stonehenge in new ways. We keep finding new clues, but does that mean we are any closer to understanding Stonehenge? Are we any better than Geoffrey of Monmouth, whose tale of Merlin building Stonehenge is illustrated on the facing page?

This is a book about questioning what others believe to be true, not accepting ideas just because famous people say they are right. I think knowledge is more like a wave than a switch. Only very rarely do we go from being totally wrong to totally

right—as a light turns off and on. Instead, what we learned before allows us to move on to what we can see next. We can surf ahead, but there will always be another challenge, another crest, another next step. We must always keep thinking and asking new questions.

Today, on this windy September morning, the tourists and the TV crew are listening to Mike. His research on Stonehenge has made headlines around the world. But Mike was not always the media star. In fact, in 1998, when he first wrote about Stonehenge, his work was greeted with doubt and uproar. And that is the really big story here—how a new idea, a new way of thinking, can go from being dismissed to capturing the attention of the world.

This picture was drawn in the 1300s and shows Merlin using his magical strength to put the stone circle in place.

A BIRD'S-EYE VIEW OF STONEHENGE

Until recently, people who studied Stonehenge looked only at the stone circle itself. The Riverside team believes that we need to understand how ancient people used the many sites shown in this map in order to make sense of Stonehenge. Here is a modern artist's idea of what a bird might have seen, flying over the Stonehenge region ca 1500 B.C. The stone circle itself rose up atop a hill. A wide avenue moved straight down the gentle slope, then angled sharply and bent to reach the River Avon. A long thin rectangle marked off in the earth, later called a "cursus," ended just before a "long barrow" burial mound. Upriver stood Durrington Walls, a huge earth circle, with several smaller circles, these made out of tall timbers, inside and just outside of the Walls. We will visit all of these sites on the following pages.

BLUESTONEHENGE

RIVER AVON

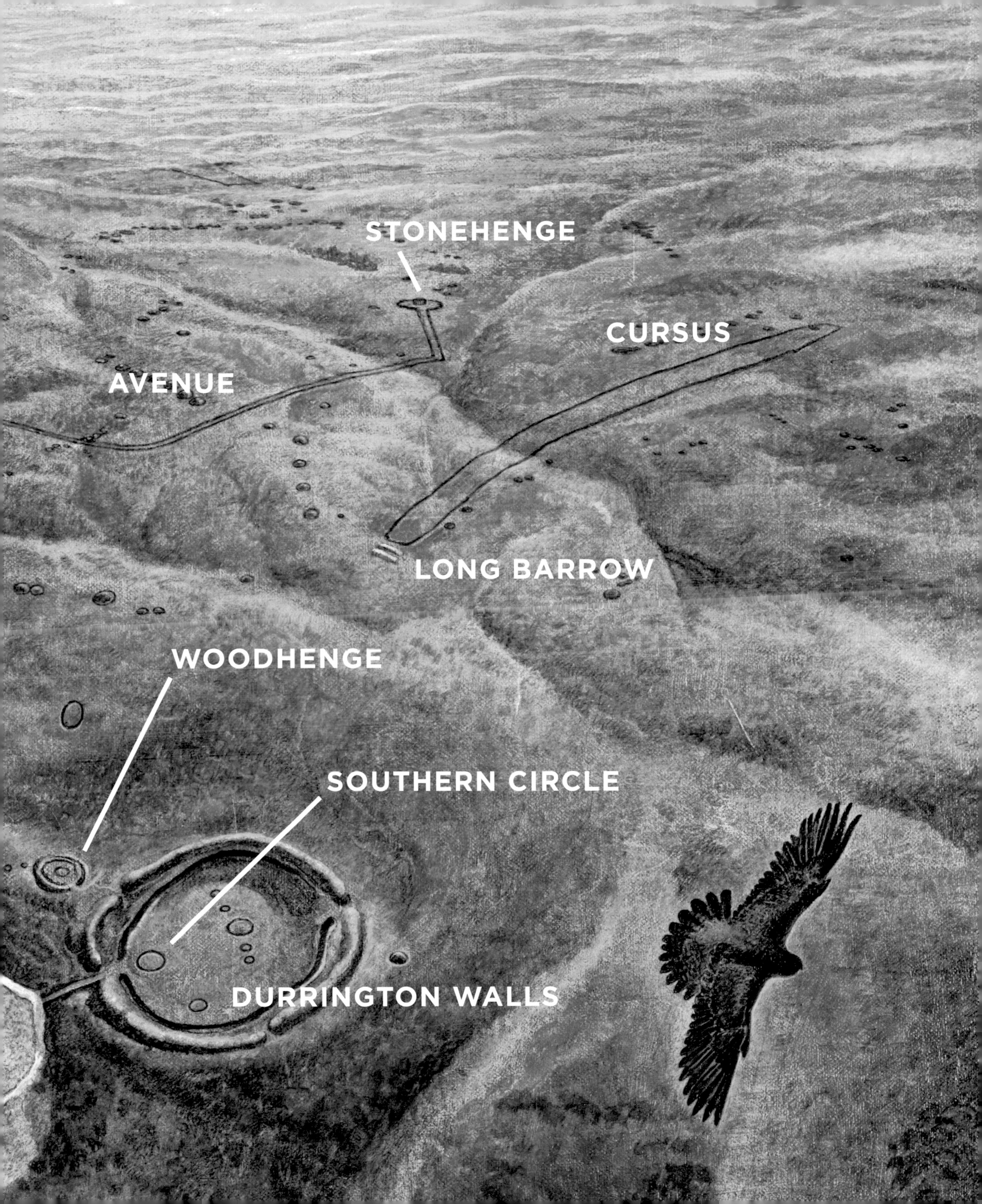

STONEHENGE

CURSUS

AVENUE

LONG BARROW

WOODHENGE

SOUTHERN CIRCLE

DURRINGTON WALLS

A TOUR AROUND STONEHENGE

WHAT YOU SEE WHEN YOU approach Stonehenge depends on how you look. A quick glance shows a circle of rather tall, grayish, chunky stones, some of which have beams called "lintels" across the top linking two neighbors—like a doorway, or an "H" with the middle line across the top. Look more carefully and you see similar stones, but fallen on the ground. These large pillars are all sarsen, a form of stone made from grains of sand that have hardened and bonded to form a tough form of sandstone. Then you may pick out some thinner, smaller stones about half the height of the taller slabs—these are made out of a different stone that can look greenish but is called bluestone. Once you identify the two kinds of stone, you may begin to notice the care and craft that went into building Stonehenge. The builders worked with stone as if it were wood.

Two bluestones stand in front of two larger sarsens, crowned by a lintel.

The two highways shown in this 1930 photograph (OPPOSITE) *have been widened and are today clogged with traffic, but Stonehenge still dominates the landscape.*

Stonehenge was designed so that on the longest day of the year the sun rises past the so-called heel stone seen here in the middle background and then through these linked sarsens.

When Stonehenge was in use, the entire outer ring of sarsens was connected by lintels. These crossing stones were held in place with a mortise and tenon joint. On the bottom of the lintel, a mortise (the carved out portion) fits over the standing sarsen's tenon (the part sticking out of the top). This is probably the same way wooden beams were attached in homes of that time and place.

Walking around Stonehenge, it is easier to see this mortise (FAR RIGHT), *which is at ground level, than the tenon* (LEFT), *which is at the top of a standing sarsen.*

Scientists have been able to determine that the heavy sarsens were all moved about 18 miles to be raised at Stonehenge; the smaller bluestones come from 150 miles away. Usually, when visitors see the stones they ask how the builders moved 35-ton rocks over hill and dale. Mike is sure we will never be able to answer that. Without writing, the builders cannot tell us, and the materials they would have used—such as sledges made out of wood or ropes made out of leather—could not survive the thousands of years of English weather. Instead of guessing how the stones were moved, archaeologists continue to ask the more interesting question: why?

WHERE THE STONES COME FROM

Most of the bluestones are made out of a distinctive form of rock called spotted dolerite. Scientists have been able to identify the rock by examining it under a microscope, as in this slide (inset). Spotted dolerite is found only in the Preseli Mountains of southwest Wales (shown below). That means the bluestones were brought, or moved by natural forces, approximately 150 miles, as shown in the map at right. Sarsen stones still lie in the fields of Marlborough Downs 18 miles north of Stonehenge.

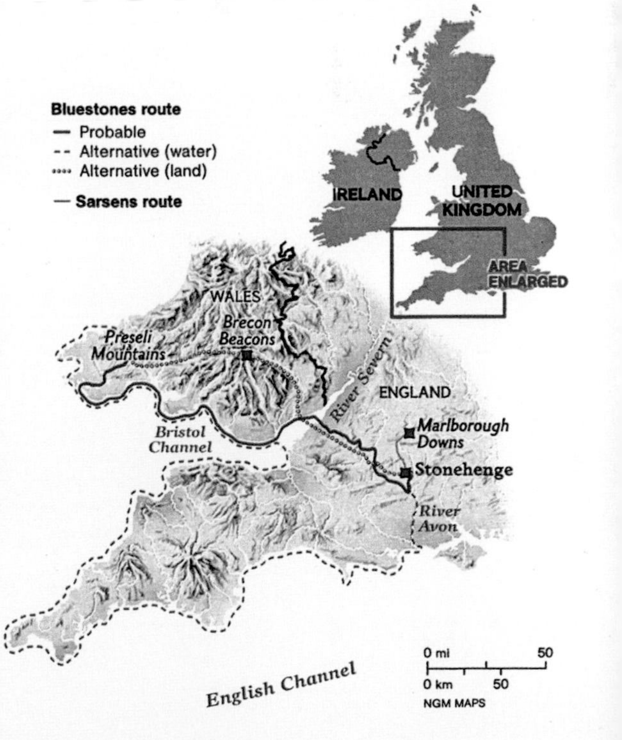

Bluestones route
— Probable
-- Alternative (water)
···· Alternative (land)

— **Sarsens route**

IRELAND

UNITED KINGDOM

AREA ENLARGED

WALES

Preseli Mountains

Brecon Beacons

River Severn

ENGLAND

Bristol Channel

Marlborough Downs

Stonehenge

River Avon

English Channel

0 mi 50
0 km 50
NGM MAPS

CHAPTER THREE

THE MAKING OF AN ARCHAEOLOGIST

I FIRST READ ABOUT MIKE IN A NEWS article that announced some of his key discoveries. But when I spoke with him, I learned that how he came to work at Stonehenge was as interesting as anything he found. He really is proof that when we look with new eyes, we can see a new past. And that is as true of you as it is of him.

Mike (with the red shirt and suspenders) examines a find in 2007 (OPPOSITE).

Mike grew up thinking he would never get to work at Stonehenge. He believed it had already been studied to death and that men far more famous than he could ever hope to be had complete control of the site.

Mike's mom did bring him to Stonehenge when he was a baby, just one year old. And as a student he took field trips to the site nearly every summer. But that is not why he set out to become an archaeologist. Instead, when he was a child growing up in Devon (in southwest England), workers who were laying a pipe near his home discovered an ancient burial site with human bones in it. Mike was fascinated. What was the story behind those bones, and how could someone figure it out? He wanted to be the kind of scientist who could dig up relics like that and make sense of them.

Mike at one year old, getting his first view of Stonehenge. Access to Stonehenge is much more restricted today.

These scrapbook photos show the life of a young archaeologist in training: visiting the ruins of a Roman villa with his family as a young teenager (TOP; MIKE IS AT RIGHT) *and, at age 24, working on a dig 18 miles south of Stonehenge* (RIGHT; MIKE IS IN THE HOLE).

When Mike reached high school, his teachers told him to be sensible. "There are no jobs in archaeology," they warned. But Mike was determined to follow the career that he had dreamed of ever since he was four years old. Whenever he had free time, even during his vacations, he found ways to be of use on archaeological sites. Soon he was helping out on one dig after another in Britain. While studying for his degree in college, he expanded his range, working on sites all around the world.

The one place Mike was sure he would not study was Stonehenge. So Mike settled in teaching archaeology at Sheffield University, and digging far—very far—from Salisbury Plain. First, he worked on the islands of the Outer Hebrides, off the west coast of Scotland. Then Mike and his wife Karen (who is an anthropologist) spent years doing research on the island of Madagascar, which is just off the coast of Africa in the Indian Ocean. That is where Mike's Stonehenge story really begins.

Mike's excavations in the Outer Hebrides included a Bronze Age settlement (TOP RIGHT AND BELOW) *and a Viking farm* (TOP LEFT AND CENTER).

CHAPTER FOUR

THE MAN FROM MADAGASCAR

Mike got to dig at the most famous site in England because he came to know a man from an island half a world away. That is the wonderful twist in the story of Stonehenge. We don't live in the world I grew up reading about—where great men from Europe and America were the only master archaeologists. Instead, it took a man from Madagascar to understand ancient England.

For most people, if they have heard of Madagascar at all, it is because of the animated movies, or because they know about the famous lemurs and other rare species that live nowhere else on Earth. But the island is also home to peoples who have had their own fascinating history. In 1991, Mike and Karen began visiting the island to study that past.

Three days' drive from the capital, Antananarivo, lies Madagascar's hot, dry southern coast. This seems like the last place people would live—even the trees grow thorns and some are poisonous. But the desert-like hills and plains hide buried remains from over a thousand years of human settlement. Each morning, Mike and his team emerged from their tents, climbed into the Land Rover, and headed out to look for archaeological

Although Madagascar is famous for its tropical forests, its extreme south suffers from severe droughts.

sites. Would they find more of the stone-walled remains of a lost civilization from a thousand years ago? Or might they

Mike worked with local archaeologist Ramilisonina (CENTER) *and his colleague Retsihisatse* (RIGHT) *in southern Madagascar.*

find remains of even older ancient camp sites where people had collected the eggshells of extinct giant elephant birds, the largest avian species that ever lived.

Back in England in 1998, after the summer's fieldwork was over, Mike got a call. A BBC TV crew was doing a documentary on Stonehenge, and the director had a brilliant idea. While people in Madagascar live in wooden houses, they build big tombs out of stone for the dead. They also set up standing stones. Perhaps, the TV director thought, a person from a society that treats stone as so important would have a fresh insight into Stonehenge.

Local people, especially the children, always joined the digs in Madagascar (BELOW).

Mike knew just the right person. Ramilisonina (he has one name) is a retired archaeologist who was born in Madagascar and has devoted his life to studying its myths, its history, and the story of its peoples. Ramilisonina had visited England once before, but he was thrilled to come back. He hadn't visited any archaeological sites on his previous trip, so Stonehenge was completely new to him. Mike was bringing a person who could see the ancient stone circle with fresh eyes.

Many of the trees in southern Madagascar have spines or are poisonous.

Ramilisonina at the West Kennet Long Barrow, a prehistoric burial mound near Avebury in England, 1998

CHAPTER FIVE

THE QUESTION

MIKE TOLD ME THAT RAMILISONINA hated the filming at Stonehenge. It was a bitterly cold English winter, and despite his warm clothes, he was freezing. How could people live here, he asked, when there were so many warmer parts of the planet? The film crew had special access to film inside Stonehenge, so it was deserted and quiet apart from the noises of filming. As darkness fell, the cameras kept rolling, even though small pools of water on the stones froze to ice. And it was just then, in the dark and cold, alone with the stones, that Mike asked the question that unlocked the secret of Stonehenge.

Mike asked Ramilisonina what he thought the stones were for. The archaeologist replied that it was obvious. The stones were put up for the ancestors. You build out of stone when you want something that will never fade away.

We live in a world of change—we are born, grow up, become adults; winter eases into spring. But, many people believe, when we die, we enter a different world. We begin a new journey in an eternal realm. Ramilisonina thought Stonehenge must have been built to usher, to welcome, the honored dead into their permanent home.

Stonehenge at night: when the BBC crew filmed Ramilisonina, the stone circle sometimes looked as wet, dark, and ominous as this (OPPOSITE).

THE TEMPLE THEORY

Three hundred years ago William Stukeley, a man who studied remnants from the past, decided that Stonehenge was a prehistoric temple. And he mistakenly assumed that the priests who used the site were Druids—people similar to the religious leaders Julius Caesar saw when Rome invaded Britain. Stukeley had no way of knowing that Stonehenge was built more than 2,000 years before Caesar's time. This 1815 illustration shows the fantasy of Stonehenge as the center of Druid ceremonies.

Stukeley was not the first person to investigate Stonehenge. In 1620, King James I and a party of his aristocratic friends ordered their men to dig a big hole in the middle of the stone circle; they hoped to find treasure but found only animal skulls. In the 1600s, a scholar named John Aubrey drew a plan of Stonehenge. He too thought it was a Druid temple. Appointed by Charles I as "the King's Antiquary," Aubrey could be called England's first professional archaeologist.

Even now, we use stone to mark a grave. So it might seem that Ramilisonina's idea was obvious. But in fact he was turning Stonehenge upside down—seeing it in exactly the opposite way from what esteemed scholars had been saying for centuries.

For over 300 years, anyone who studied Stonehenge assumed that it had been some sort of temple. Experts thought that whoever went to the trouble of creating Stonehenge must have been building a place to worship the gods, to hold ceremonies. For example, Timothy Darvill—an accomplished archaeologist who has studied the stones intensely for a decade—believes the bluestones were brought from Wales because they were believed to have healing properties. To him, the Stonehenge circle was a religious site devoted to the sun where people went to be cured.

Ramilisonina was seeing the stones completely differently. They were not most like a temple but more like a graveyard.

At first Mike laughed; he could not take the idea seriously. It was so new, so different, so unlike what generations of famous archaeologists had thought. Imagine that you are living 4,000 years from now and someone discovers an ancient basketball court. Every famous professor, every teacher, is certain that the curves and lines were put there as part of a religious ritual; experts would carefully calculate the arc above the foul line to see if it matched the path of the moon, or sun, or even a space station. And then someone from another land, someone who did not know about all those studies, walks up, takes a look, and says: People must have used this to play games. Could that outsider be right?

The Tandroy, a people who live in southern Madagascar, begin building stone tombs in the months and years after a person dies. These stone structures (BOTTOM LEFT) *are far larger than the wooden houses* (BOTTOM RIGHT) *in which the Tandroy live. Though Ramilisonina is not Tandroy, his family follows similar traditions.*

WOODHENGE AND THE SOUTHERN CIRCLE

Just over a mile from Stonehenge in Durrington is a large circular ditch and bank. Appropriately enough, this wide circle is called Durrington Walls. Just outside the earth circle of Durrington Walls, archaeologists have found traces of circles within circles of timber. Known as Woodhenge, this site, shown in the photograph above, was first spotted from the air, when a plane flew over it on December 12, 1925. Further investigation yielded postpipes, colored markings in the soil left behind by rotted wooden pillars. Modern archaeologists have placed low concrete stubs to mark those spots, but you can see what these postpipes look like in the photograph on page 29. As you walk through the circles, it is easy to picture what an impressive place

Woodhenge must have been. But there are questions we will probably never be able to answer. The wood pillars might have been carved with designs or images—as in totem poles—or possibly connected with a kind of roof.

The Woodhenge circle has been carefully dated, and it was built centuries after the large stones were put up at Stonehenge. But in 1967 the archaeologist Geoff Wainwright was given three months to excavate the area before a new road came through. He exposed the traces of two other older timber circles known simply as the Northern and Southern circles. It was the Southern Circle that Mike believed held the key to Stonehenge. *(See map on pages 10-11 for Durrington Walls, the Southern Circle, and Woodhenge.)*

postpipes

ditch

postpipes

In Madagascar, a stone building for the dead is matched with a house made of wood, where people live. Ramilisonina saw Stonehenge through the eyes of people for whom the difference between stone and wood is as clear and true as the gap between life and death. Mike realized that there might have been a similar pairing at Stonehenge. If there was a place of stone for the dead, there could also have been a second circle, made of tall timbers, for the living. He even thought he knew just where it was.

The Southern Circle, another ancient site quite near Stonehenge, had been built out of wood, but no one had seen it as terribly important. The two archaeologists quickly wrote a paper suggesting that the Southern Circle and Stonehenge were linked. Then they began waiting for someone—any one of the famous experts on Stonehenge—to test their idea.

The traces of the Southern Circle can only be seen in postholes, with their central postpipes: dark round circles in the ground left behind as timber rotted and tiny bits of soil and rock trickled down into the space where the wood once stood. The curve that cuts between two rows of postpipes was a ditch made and used thousands of years after the Southern Circle was abandoned. For scale, note that each of the three red and white measuring rods is 2 meters (2.19 yards) long.

CHAPTER SIX

MIKE'S DECISION

THERE WAS ONE BIG PROBLEM WITH the new theory linking Stonehenge and the Southern Circle: no one knew if they were from the same time period. Today, we can be sure that Christopher Columbus did not fight in World War II because we can date his life and that war. But there are no records for Stonehenge, so we have to draw conclusions from the objects we find. When Mike and Ramilisonina proposed their theory, archaeologists were getting confusing dates at Stonehenge that did not fit with the little that was known about the age of the Southern Circle.

This part of Mike's story opened my eyes. I realized that I had been completely wrong to believe that the quest to unlock the secrets of the past ended before I was born; just the opposite. In fact the scientific tools that archaeologists use to date ancient artifacts were first developed in the 1940s and have only very recently been fine-tuned. We knew hardly anything about when, say, Stonehenge was built until just 15 years ago. The timelines of ancient history in books were educated guesswork.

The archaeologist Richard Atkinson at work in Stonehenge in 1958 (OPPOSITE)

In the 1950s, archaeologist Richard Atkinson had essentially sole control over the investigation of Stonehenge. In effect the site belonged to him. He was exactly like the men I grew up reading about—elegant, wise gentlemen who knew all. Atkinson had dug near the great trilithon—the two largest stones with a third stone across the top that frame the sun on the longest and shortest days of the year. There he discovered an important feature: "There can be no doubt," he wrote, that he had found the ramp used to raise one of the stones into place. He even recovered some of the tools used by the builders—antler picks. And in 1994, the year he died, those antlers became really important.

Atkinson was a brilliant man and a skilled archaeologist who directed work at Stonehenge between 1950 and 1978. But while in this photo he takes precise measurements with measuring tape, he chose not to write up and share his research with fellow scholars. That is one reason archaeologists today are carefully reviewing his work to understand what he did and where he was right or wrong.

The ancient people who set up the stones did not know how to work with metals such as bronze or iron. So in order to dig a hole, they used the sharp antlers shed by the local red deer. Sometimes they left bits of antler behind. Those pieces of antler are real archaeological treasure because they can be dated. We can be sure when a person used the antler—the antler picks become too brittle to dig with after a few years and so were only useful as digging tools for a short while after being shed. So radiocarbon dating the antler gives a precise date for when it was used as a tool.

The antlers from Atkinson's ramp dated to somewhere between 2400 and 2100 B.C. But antlers used in raising two of the other stones were clearly older—from around 2600–2500 B.C. This simply did not make sense. Why would ancient people have done the backbreaking work of setting up a circle of large stones, linking one to another with lintels held in place by mortice and tenon joints, only to take it apart in order to add the most important stones centuries later? Wouldn't the builders have raised the stones in the center first and then surrounded them with the circle?

An antler pick found at Durrington Walls

No one could answer that question. And while there were no precise dates for the Southern Circle, the available evidence put the timbers closer to 2500 than 2100 B.C.—as much as 400 years off from the days when the solstice sunlight would have split the stones of the great trilithon.

Mike and Ramilisonina had an interesting theory that simply did not match the accepted dates for Stonehenge. Year after year went by. Mike and Karen returned to work in Madagascar. No one stepped forward either to prove Mike wrong or to resolve the seeming contradiction in the Stonehenge timeline.

What would you do if you were entrusted with a really important idea that most of the world dismissed or ignored? How would you know to trust yourself? How would you convince people to let you test your idea? Mike finally faced a stark choice: He could let Ramilisonina's insight fall into silence. Or he could take up the challenge himself. No one else would do it for him.

In 2002 Mike took fellow archaeologist Colin Richards to see Durrington Walls. Together they hatched a plan. They would gather a team of archaeologists they had known since they were students together, call themselves the Riverside Project, and tackle the mysteries of Stonehenge. But Mike was worried. The authorities responsible for the area see their mission as protecting England's heritage, preserving as much of the landscape as possible. So why would they ever agree to let a newcomer dig at the most famous site in England? Who would agree to fund a project that turned accepted ideas upside down? Who did he think he was?

Colin Richards and Mike (shown here in 2007) have worked together in digs from Stonehenge to Easter Island.

Every day was nerve-wracking. When the officials who gave out permits to dig seemed interested in Mike's work, he could not find the money. Indeed his application for funding was turned down, and his project was called "too speculative." Yet when he caught the ear of sponsors, the officials hesitated. Nobody wanted to budge. Finally Mike got word that he could start a tiny dig in a spot no one thought important. The Project could crack the earth—but the real test was in the soil. They would find some evidence to back Mike and Ramilisonina's idea, or they would have to close up shop and go home.

CHAPTER SEVEN

THE LOST VILLAGE

THE YEAR OF DECISION WAS 2005. The year before, Mike thought his crew had made a key find when they uncovered an ancient ditch near the Southern Circle. He was certain this was the side of an avenue leading down to the River Avon *(see map on pages 10-11)*. But when they took a closer look, the ditch dated from 2,000 years after the circle. Mike was "desperately disappointed." The team found some "moderately interesting" evidence here and there, but nothing big. Another dry season of digging and the game was over.

While busloads of visitors were walking around the stone circle at Stonehenge, the Riverside team spent their days in a meadow accompanied by cows. Indeed, cows were a big problem because the farmer who owned the pasture needed a place for his herd to graze. When I came to visit, we had to step around cow patties and circle past the rather puzzled and put-out bulls. But Mike was sure this site held one of the secrets of Stonehenge.

Watching the Riverside team at work, I realized that their training allows them to read soil the way the rest of us read books.

Mike kneels on the plaster floor of one of the nine houses found between 2005 and 2007. Just in front of him is the bowl-like depression that served as a hearth. The small holes surrounding the plaster floor are the remains of the poles that framed the wooden house. On Mike's left, just outside the house, is a pit dug through the floor when the house was abandoned and filled with garbage from a final feast (OPPOSITE).

An artist's reconstruction of the house shown on page 36 as it would have looked 4,500 years ago. You can see the same plaster floor, hearth, postholes, and frame.

As Mike explained, they study how earth, rocks, and wood age and decay. So as they scrape away at a dig, they are turning pages, until in an area where you or I would see a road, or a hill, or a meadow, they can picture an ancient landscape.

If Mike was right and the giant stands of wood that had formed the Southern Circle signaled the realm of the living, people must have left traces behind. Stonehenge itself has almost no remains showing that it was used by people—just a few handfuls of broken pots and animal bones, sparse remnants of food they might have eaten in a ceremony. The team was looking for any evidence that people had once lived here, near the timber circle. In 2004 they had cut one trench and found nothing. They tried another. No luck. Now it was August of 2005, and Mike was alone on the site with a driver whose backhoe stripped off the top layer of soil on a new location. Pay dirt: black soil filled with animal bones, scraps of pottery and flint. At that moment Mike knew they had "found something fantastic. It was brilliantly exciting." Mike and the driver were looking at clear evidence that people had lived, worked, and eaten right there. And the black soil was only the start.

There beneath the grass were the remains of nine small houses surrounded by those layers full of animal bones and pottery. At first this might not seem so exciting: all that remained of the houses was their floors. The roofs and walls

Examining bones like these found near the houses, the Riverside team learned that the ancient people cooked so many animals that they could afford to be wasteful. They did not scrape bones to get every bit of meat and fat as a hungry person might. The mounds of bones that showed signs of having been thrown away when only partially eaten confirmed that the area arround the Southern Circle was used for huge feasts.

had long ago collapsed and vanished. Yet the shape of the buildings is so clear, it is almost like looking at a building plan. The team concluded that these nine houses were just a small part of a much larger settlement surrounding the Southern Circle, perhaps as many as 1,000 houses originally. If so, this was the largest Neolithic village in all of northern Europe.

Finding those houses was like opening a door and suddenly discovering an entirely new world, parallel to our own. The houses, the signs of a vast settlement, were the first real evidence ever found of where and how people lived when they used Stonehenge. Following Ramilisonina's insight about wood and stone, the Riverside team stripped away the ground cover and saw clear evidence of the land of the living: the missing half of the Stonehenge story.

This overhead shot shows more detail in one of the houses near the Southern Circle. At Skara Brae in the Orkney Islands of Scotland, archaeologists found similar homes from the same time as the Southern Circle. Because there were no trees in Orkney, the houses had stone furniture. The Durrington Walls houses had similar furniture in wood, whose only surviving traces were long straight slots to hold the beams that formed the edges of beds and dressers.

Mike has said that finding these houses was the most satisfying part of the whole Stonehenge dig.

The animal bones told a story almost as exciting as the houses. When archaeologists examined the teeth of the animals, they learned two crucial things: The pigs were typically about nine months old when they died; since pigs give birth in the spring, they must have been cooked and eaten at midwinter. The cows' teeth were more difficult to age, but the strontium in them is certainly not from the chalk soils of Durrington Walls and Stonehenge. The animals came from at least 30 miles away, and some were brought from over 70 miles away. This was not a village where farmers raised animals to eat as needed. Rather it was a special place where, once a year in the dead of winter and perhaps also in midsummer, people from a wide area gathered to feast. It was, just as Ramilisonina had expected, a place of the living—where people held celebrations.

But what did they celebrate?

CHAPTER EIGHT

THE ALIGNMENT, AND THE MISTAKE

TODAY, SOME 35,000 PEOPLE TRAVEL to Stonehenge on the longest day of the year (which is generally June 21). On that day, and that day only, the rays of the rising sun color the avenue and then split the pillars of the great trilithon. The summer solstice, as it is called, is captured in light and stone. But those who built Stonehenge did not just stand within the stone circle.

The ditch between the Southern Circle and the River Avon that the team found in 2004 proved to be a false lead. The following year they discovered the real avenue—a roadway so important that the people who built it paved it with flint. And that avenue revealed one more secret of Stonehenge.

Mike and his team discovered that a person standing at the Avon at the end of that same midsummer's day would have seen the light of the setting sun moving up the avenue into the Southern Circle. Linking the two circles was the river. People would have seen the sunrise in stone and walked along the river, timing their passage to arrive at the wooden circle for sunset.

Tourists and believers still flock to Stonehenge at the midsummer solstice—as they did in this photo taken in 1958 (OPPOSITE).

Looking carefully at this picture, you can see the 50-foot-wide avenue that ran from the Southern Circle to the Avon. The two men in red and the yellow buckets at the center are standing in the middle of the dark flint-paved avenue. The avenue has a low chalk ridge on each side, visible as lighter ground.

On the shortest day of winter, the pattern reverses. A person standing within the wood circle and looking out the entrance would see the sun rising up the avenue. Facing the sun as it rises, he or she would walk along the Avon, timing the passage to arrive at Stonehenge at sunset, where the sun's rays would once again split the great trilithon. The two circles were set, like the gears in a watch, to work together, to fix two points in two crucial days. The turning of the entire year was marked by Stonehenge and the Southern Circle. To this day, when Mike talks about this discovery, you can see the sense of wonder in his eyes.

AVENUE

Andrew Chamberlain, a colleague of Mike's at Sheffield University, uses a laser to create a 3-D computer model of the carefully dug and packed hole which once held a standing stone at Bluestonehenge. The river that linked the lands of the living and of the dead is beginning to give up its secrets.

Mike had to explain this to me many times, but when I finally got it, I literally felt the ground shifting under my feet. Back to the basketball court: it is as if scholars had been spending all of their time trying to make sense of one basket and someone figured out that there was another on the opposite end. Suddenly the whole space would matter, not just one goal. In fact that is exactly what happened, as the Riverside team studied the river linking the two circles.

In the 1930s and 1940s, archaeologists found two locations along the riverside where there were pits filled with ash—the remains of giant bonfires. Upstream, next to Durrington Walls and Woodhenge, the team discovered another three wooden monuments along the river cliff, perhaps with high platforms from which the ancient people looked down at the river. In 2009, at the Stonehenge end, they made the thrilling discovery of Bluestonehenge: a circle of bluestones, originally from Wales, that once stood here beside the riverbank *(see map on pages 10–11)*. This site may have been the original home of some of the taller bluestones now forming the inner circle at Stonehenge.

Josh Pollard led the excavations at Woodhenge and also found remains of raised timber platforms south of Woodhenge, overlooking the River Avon.

Unfortunately, we cannot experience the journey today as the ancient people did. A raised roadway blocks the sightlines to and from the Southern Circle. But we can imagine it, picture it in our minds. And in doing so we can begin to understand Stonehenge as part of an environment in which people lived: a timber circle on one end, with an avenue to a river; a river flowing along to another avenue leading up to a circle of stone. As Ramilisonina had understood, Stonehenge was part of a landscape marking off the land of the living from the land of the dead.

For hundreds of years, everyone who tried to understand Stonehenge was hypnotized by the circle of stones. Ramilisonina's sense that stone must be paired with wood broke the spell. Suddenly we can look up, look around, and picture how people lived here thousands of years ago.

The work of an archaeologist is not all digging in trenches. Sometimes the most important clues can be found in archives and libraries.

In 2005, the Riverside team was making great discoveries on the ground, but what about those puzzling dates for Stonehenge and the mismatch with the Southern Circle? After the year's digging was over, Mike went to the files to carefully review Atkinson's records. There he discovered that the great man had made a mistake. What he took to be a ramp could not have been used that way because it did not actually come

later ditch

bluestones

later ditch

close enough to the hole where the stone ended up. In fact, one of Atkinson's assistants had noticed this error—but he was too afraid to speak up. Atkinson's announcement that there could be "no doubt" silenced him.

With that error cleared up, the new date for the raising of the sarsens at Stonehenge was between 2600 and 2480 B.C. The central stones that frame the sun and the outer circle were put up at the same time, around 2500 B.C. Dates taken from antler picks dug out from the Southern Circle show it was built between 2500 and 2480 B.C. The dates are a perfect match.

Bluestonehenge: Bluestones once stood where you see team members in their colorful shirts (only part of the circle has been excavated). The bluestones were later removed (probably to Stonehenge) and the site was enclosed with a ditch and bank.

CHAPTER NINE

THE STORY WE CAN NOW TELL

THE RIVERSIDE TEAM IS NOW confident of the big picture. Stonehenge is just one point in a much larger map—which included places to feast, perhaps to celebrate, and places to bury the dead.

I felt that shift in focus very clearly as I looked at the work being done all over the Stonehenge region by the team. The three great discoveries in 2005—the houses, the bones, and the true avenue—captured the attention of the world, and the team got permission to spread out. What they are finding is changing Stonehenge from a mystery into a story.

We do not know why the builders of Stonehenge went to the trouble to bring bluestones from faraway Wales. One possibility is that the early farmers who may have first moved to Salisbury Plain around 3800 B.C. came from Wales. Perhaps they went back to bring stones to link them with their place of origin. Mike plans to explore this theory by using the same tests that told us where the animals eaten at the Southern Circle were raised. Inside Boles Barrow, a burial mound 11 miles west of Stonehenge, diggers found a half-ton bluestone. Could this be a hint of a link between people and

Julian Thomas of the Riverside team digs at the west end of the Cursus (OPPOSITE).

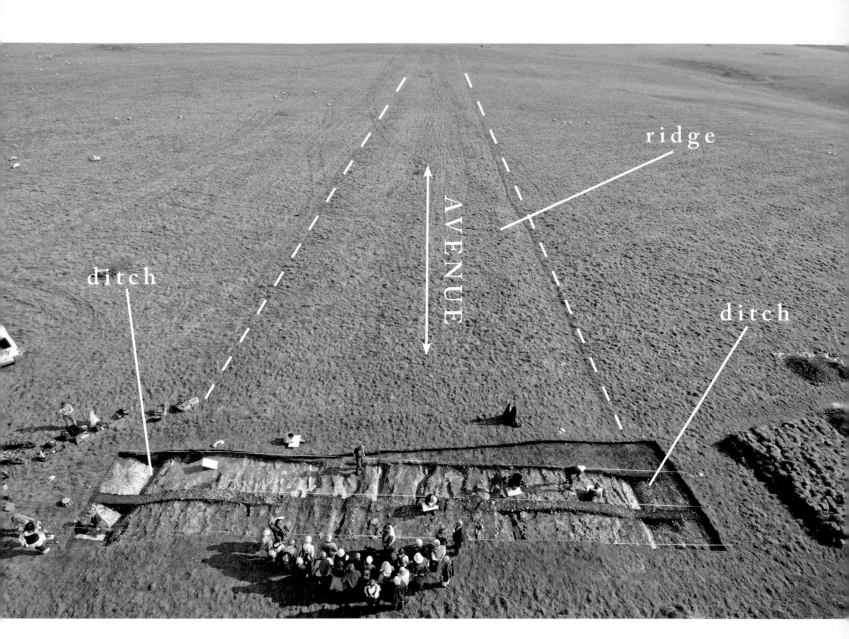

ridge

AVENUE

ditch

ditch

place? A strontium isotope analysis of the teeth from the skulls found in the barrow should tell us where those people came from. The remains of what looks like a huge feast also held around 3800 B.C. were found at another nearby site called Coneybury Hill. While the strontium tests at Boles Barrow will tell us about people, the same test at Coneybury may give us information about their cattle. Those two tests could provide the key connection among early farmers, their animals, the bluestones, and Wales.

The Riverside team found evidence of the next act in the story in a feature called the Cursus *(see map on pages 10-11)*. The Cursus is a very long, thin rectangle—1.8 miles (2.9 kilometers) in length and about 480 feet (146 meters) across—bounded by a ditch and bank. The ditch and bank had been investigated four times, but nothing turned up that scientists could date. In 2007, Julian Thomas found an antler pick that finally gave a date: the Cursus was built between 3600 and 3300 B.C. Already then this area was important enough to be marked off.

I had the good luck to be standing there when Charly French and Mike Allen—who are friends of the Riverside team and experts on reconstructing how a place looked thousands of years ago—came up with an idea that may explain the next phase of building and why Stonehenge is where it is.

This is the antler pick that finally allowed the team to date the Cursus and begin to put together the real chronology of the Stonehenge region.

There are many natural ridges in the landscape near Stonehenge. On the gentle hill leading down from Stonehenge, two of these ridges form parallel lines. In June of a dry summer, Charly and Mike suggested, not much grass would grow, so the shape of the land would be clearly visible. Perhaps on one midsummer's day, a person saw the rising sun inching along the ridge lines to the top of the hill. On that one special day, the sun rose exactly along those straight lines. Maybe the ripples suggested the avenue and pointed to the place for the ring and the stones. Indeed we know that the avenue on that hillside was later formed by adding earth on top of the natural ridges *(for Stonehenge avenue, see map on pages 10-11)*.

The new idea that natural ridges in the soil may have suggested the site for the avenue and for Stonehenge on the top of the hillside opens up other possibilities. Archaeologists have long known that some 10,000 years ago giant posts were set in the ground near where the stone circle would later be built. Could it be that there was another "natural monument" here? Perhaps this site was considered special for 5,000 years before Stonehenge was built. The team has found traces of where the builders of those earliest posts lived, down by the river.

Mike and the team digging in an Aubrey Hole at Stonehenge itself in 2008 (OPPOSITE). *They found cremation burials from all phases of Stonehenge.*

The first stage of building on Stonehenge itself came some 400 years after the Cursus, around 3000 B.C. The team learned more about this phase when it investigated the Aubrey Holes, the 56 holes discovered by John Aubrey in 1666. The Welsh bluestones were placed in these holes to form a wide circle inside the bank in 3000-2935 B.C., long before anyone had thought. And Stonehenge was used for burials right from this moment for

the next 700 years—the largest cemetery anywhere in Britain at that time. The team found that human cremation burials were placed within the Aubrey Holes in which the bluestones first stood, even within the packed chalk that held them upright. From the first, Stonehenge was a home for the honored dead.

From 2500 B.C. on we have the story that the team discovered in 2005—the place of living and feasting near the Southern Circle just as the stone circle for the dead was completed at Stonehenge.

And then it all ended. Mike thinks that the homes he found, and many others, were deliberately closed down, covered in dirt. When people stopped using the stone circle, they did not need the feasting place of the wooden circle. But they recalled what their ancestors had done, and turned the whole area into a giant memorial: an enclosure with a ditch on the inside and a bank on the outside—as if to keep something inside the circle.

Why? Why did the rituals of timber and stone end? There are hints in some of the excavations in the area. Around 2300 B.C., a man who had grown up in Switzerland was buried near Stonehenge, in what is now Amesbury. He was buried with gold—the earliest gold found in England—as well as copper. Perhaps, as people skilled in the use of metals like copper and bronze arrived in England, the old ways of living changed. Instead of working together in large groups to raise stones or hold feasts, people broke up into smaller bands. The great stone circle was left to stand on its own, with no processions, no new burials. The place of ceremonies slowly turned into the mute message from the distant past. The stones went silent.

The Amesbury skeleton and his hoard of metal blades and stone tools (OPPOSITE)

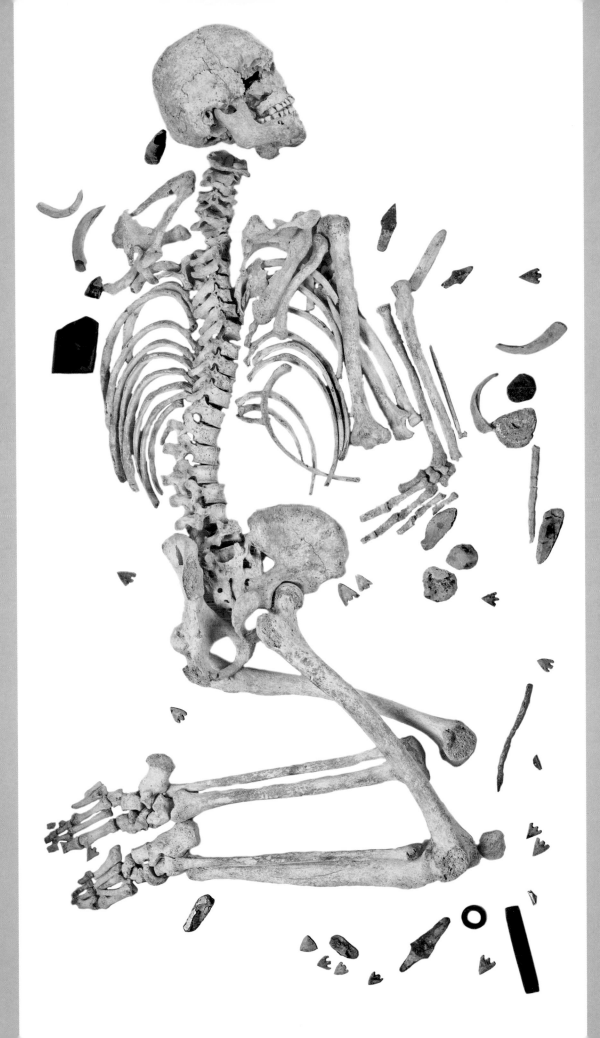

SEEING STONEHENGE

THIS IS A BOOK about Ramilisonina and Mike, but not only about them. Really it is about putting aside what you think you know, what has been passed along, and being willing to trust what you yourself see and to test it rigorously. On July 10, 1953, Richard Atkinson was waiting for just the right light to take a photo of one of the stones. Suddenly he saw carvings on it, a cluster of what looked like axe heads and a dagger. The carvings had always been there, but no one had observed them. A few days later a boy, ten years old, noticed more axe head carvings on other stones. It is not just that the boy had good eyesight, he had a willingness to look in a new way. The carvings did not "solve" Stonehenge—but they came from seeing with clear eyes, and a boy was as capable of doing that as the most famous archaeologist in England.

When the BBC crew invited Ramilisonina to Stonehenge, they were ending the era in which one single archaeologist could be the voice of the past. They were opening the analysis of Stonehenge out to the world. Similarly, several team members told me that digging all over the planet is what gives them new insight into Stonehenge. Today, the team working in the area includes over 30 professional archaeologists. While Mike most often speaks to the press, that is really just a matter of convenience. All of the scientists are experts, and they question each other, challenge each other's views. The results Mike announces represent their collective best efforts. We are seeing more in Stonehenge because more people are looking, and in more ways.

Kate Welham directs the geophysical survey and electronic recording of all the sites investigated by the Riverside team. Here she is using a portable global positioning system.

Dr. Mike Allen: An expert on geoarchaeology, which is the study of what a landscape must have been long ago based on traces of evidence found today. After working at Wessex Archaeology for 18 years, he now runs Allen Environment Archaeology. *See pages 51 and 52.*

Amesbury Archer: The skeleton of a man determined to have grown up in what is now Switzerland around 2300 B.C., found buried near Stonehenge, along with a rich pile of grave goods that indicate he was wealthy and practiced archery. *See pages 54, 55, and 63.*

Richard Atkinson (1920–1994): The main authority on Stonehenge from 1950 to 1978 and author of what was long considered the best popular book on the stones. His work is now being reexamined and questioned. *See pages 31, 32, 33, 46, 47, 56, 62, and 64. See also boxes,* Archaeologists and Their Theories *(this page) and* Chronology of the Riverside Project's Digs In and Around Stonehenge *(opposite).*

Aubrey Holes: Fifty-six holes inside the bank at Stonehenge that were first described in 1666 by John Aubrey. In 2008, the Riverside team found new evidence that cremated bones and standing stones were placed in the holes long before the sarsen stones were raised at Stonehenge. *See pages 52, 54, and 63. See also box,* Chronology of the Riverside Project's Digs In and Around Stonehenge *(opposite).*

John Aubrey (1626–1697): Britain's first great archaeologist. Aubrey is best remembered today as the author of *Brief Lives*, a collection of biographical sketches. During his study of Stonehenge in 1666, he discovered what became known as the Aubrey Holes. *See page 26. See also box,* Archaeologists and Their Theories *(this page).*

Avon: A word that meant "river" in the ancient language spoken in what is now Britain before the Romans invaded. As a result, there are several Avon rivers in Britain today. The Avon near Stonehenge is not the same as the river that runs through Stratford, where Shakespeare was born. *See pages 10–11, 37, 43, 44, 45, 46, 47, and 63.*

Bluestone: The smaller of the two kinds of stone used at Stonehenge. Tests have determined that many of the bluestones came from the Preseli Hills in Wales, some 150 miles away. *See pages 13, 15, 27, 49, 50, 52, 54, and 63.*

Bluestonehenge: *See* Stonehenge II *(page 61).*

Boles Barrow: A burial mound 11 miles from Stonehenge, dating to ca 3800–3400 B.C. It was excavated 200 years ago, when a bluestone was reportedly found in the mound. *See pages 49 and 50.*

Hiram Bingham (1875–1956): An American archaeologist most famous for locating Machu Picchu, the "lost city of the Incas." *See page 8.*

Bronze Age: In Britain, a period of history that dates from 2200 B.C. to 700 B.C. Scholars often define a historical period by the materials used at the time. The Stone Age (itself split into "old" or Paleolithic, "middle" or Mesolithic, and "new" or Neolithic) was followed by the Bronze Age and the Iron Age. Stonehenge was built at the end of the Neolithic period. Copper tools and weapons were introduced to Britain ca 2500 B.C. *See pages 19 and 64.*

ARCHAEOLOGISTS AND THEIR THEORIES

1666 John Aubrey identified Stonehenge as ancient British, built as a temple for the Druids. He discovered Stonehenge's outer circle of pits, named after him as the Aubrey Holes.

1721-24 William Stukeley described and drew Stonehenge and its surrounding monuments. He agreed with Aubrey that Stonehenge was a Druid temple. He discovered the Stonehenge avenue in 1721.

1874-77 William Flinders-Petrie, the famous Egyptologist, made a very accurate plan of Stonehenge. His theory that it was a prehistoric royal burial ground is now supported by new evidence recovered in 2008.

1877 Charles Darwin and his children dug two holes in Stonehenge to find out how earthworms move soil over long periods of time.

1901 William Gowland, a geologist, excavated Stonehenge's giant trilithon during restoration works. Published a year later, his exemplary records were the best for Stonehenge within the 20th century.

1919-1926 William Hawley dug most of the eastern half of Stonehenge, much of it on his own, and failed to publish a full account of his discoveries. He ended up more puzzled by Stonehenge than when he started.

1950-1978 Richard Atkinson dug inside Stonehenge and along its avenue. He thought Stonehenge was built as a temple, influenced by Mycenaeans from prehistoric Greece. Although Atkinson was considered a leading excavator in his day, his records were worse than Hawley's, whom he criticized for poor work.

Bulford Standing Stone: A sarsen located a few miles from Stonehenge that lies on its side at the center of a ring ditch. *See box,* Chronology of the Riverside Project's Digs In and Around Stonehenge *(this page).*

Julius Caesar (100–44 B.C.): Roman general and later emperor, he conquered Gaul (France) and invaded Britain. Caesar wrote about his conquests, and later readers mistakenly assumed that the Britons he fought were similar to the builders of Stonehenge—2,500 years before his time. *See page 26.*

Carbon-14 and carbon-12: Isotopes of carbon. The element carbon is found in all living things but comes in various forms or isotopes, depending on how many neutrons are present. Carbon-14 begins to lose its extra neutrons and change into carbon-12 as soon as an organism dies. *See pages 33 and 41.*

Coneybury Hill: A site near Stonehenge where archaeologists found a large pit filled with remains of a huge feast held around 3800 B.C. *See page 50.*

Cuckoo Stone: A single sarsen near Stonehenge. Colin Richards of the Riverside team has established that this sarsen was not moved to its current site but has lain there since ancient times. It once stood upright, next to a pit in which an antler pick was carefully buried ca 2900 B.C. *See box,* Chronology of the Riverside Project's Digs In and Around Stonehenge *(this page).*

Cursus: The Latin word for "race track." In the 1700s, when William Stukeley saw the large rectangular marking in the earth near Stonehenge, he thought it must have been a Roman race track. The Riverside team has proven that the Cursus near Stonehenge was built before Stonehenge and thousands of years before the Romans arrived. *See pages 10–11, 49, 51, 52, and 63. See box,* Chronology of the Riverside Project's Digs In and Around Stonehenge *(this page).*

Dr. Timothy Darvill: An archaeologist at Bournemouth University who has devoted a lifetime of study to Stonehenge. He believes it was a center of healing, not a place for the honored dead. *See pages 26, 62, and 64.*

Charles Darwin (1809–1882): The great naturalist and father of evolutionary theory. *See box,* Archaeologists and Their Theories *(opposite).*

Druids: The religious leaders of the people living in Britain at the time of Caesar's invasions in 55 and 54 B.C. Little is known about these priests. The believers who call themselves Druids today claim a link to those ancient ways, but their beliefs and practices are modern inventions. *See pages 8 and 26.*

Durrington Walls: A very large, 1,400-foot-wide enclosure surrounded by a high bank and 20-foot-deep ditch. This giant henge was built on the former site of a large settlement with

CHRONOLOGY OF **THE RIVERSIDE PROJECT'S** DIGS IN AND AROUND STONEHENGE

This box outlines all of the Riverside team's work in the Stonehenge area, including activities not discussed in this book. For more detailed information, visit the Riverside Project pages at the University of Sheffield website *(see* Online Resources, *page 64).*

2003. Durrington Walls: tree and shrub clearance, surveys and tests.

2004. Durrington Walls: digs near river and outside henge.

2005. Durrington Walls avenue and houses; Southern Circle; Larkhill (a Neolithic site north of Stonehenge); Bulford standing stone. Discovery of Atkinson's mistake at Stonehenge *(see pages 46–47).*

2006. Durrington Walls avenue and houses; Durrington Walls interior; Woodhenge; Fargo plantation (a Neolithic site near the Cursus). Completion of three-year landscape survey of monuments around Stonehenge; completion of geophysical survey at Durrington Walls.

2007. Durrington Walls houses, banks, west and south entrances; timber buildings south of Woodhenge; the Cuckoo Stone; east end of the Cursus; former channel of River Avon. Rediscovery, from William Hawley's notes, that the Aubrey Holes held standing stones.

2008. Stonehenge; Stonehenge avenue; Stonehenge palisade; Stonehenge dressing floor; west end of Cursus and Long Barrow; Stonehenge avenue "extension"; riverside end of Stonehenge avenue; Fargo plantation. Strontium isotope results for Stonehenge cattle; radiocarbon dates for Durrington Walls. Discovery of Stukeley drawing that suggests the route by which the sarsens were brought to Stonehenge.

2009. Riverside end of the Stonehenge avenue reveals holes of a stone circle that once held bluestones. There may have been 22 stones in this circle. Radiocarbon dates for Stonehenge avenue and Cursus long barrow.

2010. Radiocarbon dates for the people buried at Stonehenge.

timber circles, the Southern and Northern circles. *See pages 8, 10–11, 33, 34, 40, 41, 45, and 63.*

Elephant birds: The largest birds in the world, these 10-foot-tall flightless birds laid huge eggs, equivalent to over 200 chickens' eggs, and lived in Madagascar but have been extinct since at least the 1600s. *See page 22.*

William Flinders-Petrie (1853–1942): A British archaeologist known for his careful and precise studies of ancient sites. He began studying Stonehenge when he was just 21 and did his most famous work in Egypt. *See box,* Archaeologists and Their Theories *(page 58).*

Dr. Charly French: Director of the McBurney Laboratory for Geoarchaeology at Cambridge. He is an expert on recovering "buried landscapes"—reconstructing the ancient terrain and vegetation from long ago. *See pages 51 and 52.*

Geoffrey of Monmouth (ca 1100–1155): Author of the *History of the Kings of Britain,* an early source for many stories of King Arthur and Merlin, including the legend that Merlin had the stones sent from Ireland to Stonehenge. His work is now seen as more legend and fantasy than actual history. *See pages 8 and 64.*

William Gowland (1842–1922): Worked as a mining engineer in Japan, where he also investigated ancient archaeological sites. During his work at Stonehenge in 1901, he meticulously recorded his findings. *See box,* Archaeologists and Their Theories *(page 58).*

William Hawley (1851–1941): Did extensive work at Stonehenge, excavating most of its eastern half between 1919 and 1926. *See boxes,* Archaeologists and Their Theories *(page 58) and* Chronology of the Riverside Project's Digs In and Around Stonehenge *(page 59).*

Henge: A name scholars have given to circular earthworks characterized by a ditch and a bank. In most henges, the ditch is inside of the bank, while the opposite is true at Stonehenge. Henges have been dated to the Neolithic and Bronze ages, some 5,000–3,000 years ago, but scholars are not certain how they were used. *See pages 7 and 47.*

Isotopes: Variant forms of chemical elements that have more or fewer neutrons but the same number of protons. *See pages 33, 41, and 50.*

Lintel: A crossing beam supported by columns on either side. *See pages 13, 14, and 33.*

Madagascar: The fourth largest island in the world and the 46th largest country, it is in the Indian Ocean, off the east coast of Africa. *See pages 19, 21, 22, 23, 27, 29, and 34.*

Merlin: The storied advisor to King Arthur who was said to have mastered magical powers. Merlin appears in many myths, legends, and fantasy novels. *See pages 8 and 9.*

Mortise and tenon joint: At Stonehenge, and probably in wooden houses from the same period, the method used to hold lintels in place: a projection (or tenon) from an upright sarsen is fitted into a facing hole (or mortise) on the underside of the lintel. *See pages 14 and 33.*

Neolithic: A term meaning "new Stone Age," lasting in Britain from 4000 B.C. to 2500 B.C. This was when farming was introduced to hunter-gatherers of the Mesolithic, or "middle," Stone Age. *See page 40.*

Old English: The language spoken in Britain from the 400s to around 1100, when the language began to change under the influence of the French spoken by William the Conqueror and his followers. *See page 7.*

Orkney (also known as the Orkney Islands): A group of islands north of Scotland in which people have lived for at least 9,000 years. Skara Brae, a village inhabited from 3200 to 2500 B.C., is the best preserved Neolithic settlement in Europe. *See page 40.*

Outer Hebrides: An island group off the west coast of Scotland whose many prehistoric remains include the 5,000-year-old stone circle of Calanais. *See page 19.*

Radiocarbon dating: A method for dating ancient artifacts that contain carbon. Since carbon-14 begins to decay into carbon-12 when an organism dies, and scientists know how long it takes for this change to take place, they can date any artifact containing carbon by how much carbon-14 is left. However, objects older than 40,000 years have lost their carbon-14 and must be dated in other ways. *See page 33.*

Ramilisonina: An archaeologist from Madagascar. During his visit to Stonehenge in 1998, he suggested that its stones symbolized the eternal permanence of the ancestors, in contrast to the perishable wooden circles for the living; this insight led to the Riverside Project's studies. *See pages 22, 23, 25, 26, 27, 29, 31, 34, 35, 40, 41, 46, 56, and 57.*

Retsihisatse: A colleague of Ramilisonina's who lives in southern Madagascar. *See page 22.*

Riverside Project (team): A group of archaeologists and researchers, led by Mike Parker Pearson, that has been studying Stonehenge and other ancient sites on Salisbury Plain. *See pages 8, 33, 34, 37, 39, 40, 45, 46, 49, 51, 57, and 62. See also boxes,* The Riverside Project Team *(opposite) and* Chronology of the Riverside Project's Digs In and Around Stonehenge *(page 59).*

Salisbury Plain: Plateau formed of chalk in south central England that includes the region around Stonehenge. *See pages 7, 19, 49, and 63.*

Sarsen: A tough form of sandstone. The large stones at Stonehenge are all sarsen, and many may have come from about 18 miles to the north. *See pages 13, 14, 15, 47, and 63.*

Heinrich Schliemann (1822–1890): A German who was certain that Troy, as mentioned in the ancient Greek epic poems the *Iliad* and the *Odyssey,* was a real place. While many faults have been found with his work, he did link the legendary city with a real and important site. *See page 8.*

Solstice (summer and winter solstices): One of two times a year when the sun is at its greatest angle to the equator. At the summer solstice, around June 21, the longest day in the Northern Hemisphere, the sun is above the Tropic of Cancer. At the winter solstice, around December 22, the shortest day in the Northern Hemisphere, it is above the Tropic of Capricorn. One of the most intriguing discoveries made by the Riverside team was how the rising and setting suns of the solstices link Stonehenge and the Southern Circle. *See pages 34 and 43.*

Southern Circle: A timber circle located within Durrington Walls that the Riverside team believes is linked to Stonehenge. *See pages 10–11, 28, 29, 31, 34, 37, 38, 39, 40, 43, 44, 46, 47, 49, 54, and 63. See also box,* Chronology of the Riverside Project's Digs In and Around Stonehenge *(page 59).*

Stonehenge II (now called Bluestonehenge): First thought to be a small henge, now known to have once held a circle of standing bluestones. *See pages 10–11, 45, 47, and 63.*

Stonehenge avenue: An ancient avenue from Stonehenge almost two miles long, aligned on the summer solstice sunrise until turning at its "elbow" to lead to the River Avon. *See pages 10–11, 43, 45, 46, 47, 50, and 52.*

Stonehenge dressing floor: The area outside Stonehenge's main entrance where the sarsens received their final shaping, or dressing, before they were put up. It was found in 2008 by the Riverside Project. *See box,* Chronology of the Riverside Project's Digs In and Around Stonehenge *(page 59).*

Stonehenge palisade: A Bronze Age land boundary that runs northeast-southwest past the west side of Stonehenge. *See box,* Chronology of the Riverside Project's Digs In and Around Stonehenge *(page 59).*

Strontium analysis: A method for determining the geographic origin of the bones and teeth that archaeologists uncover in their excavations. Strontium is a mineral that can be measured in bones and teeth. One quirk about strontium is that the blend of strontium isotopes found in the ground varies from place to place. Scientists have learned to use this knowledge to identify, from the teeth they find, where a particular animal or person may have come from. *See pages 41 and 50.*

William Stukeley (1687–1765): After John Aubrey, the first important investigator of Stonehenge. Stukeley was a doctor who made frequent trips to the ancient site to survey, measure, and make careful drawings. In 1740, he published his findings in *Stonehenge, a Temple Restor'd to the British Druids. See pages 26 and 64. See also box,* Archaeologists and Their Theories *(page 58).*

Trilithon: A structure in which two large vertical stones support a third horizontal stone lain across the top. The inner circle of Stonehenge consists of five trilithons in a horseshoe arrangement. *See pages 32, 34, 43, and 44.*

Troy: Once thought to be a legendary city known only in the *Iliad* and the *Odyssey*, Homer's tales of the Trojan War. A site near the coast of northwest Turkey is now considered to be the historical Troy. *See page 8.*

Tandroy: The name of the ethnic group that lives in the extreme south of Madagascar. *See pages 22 and 27.*

Woodhenge: An ancient site located just outside Durrington Walls that consists of traces of circles within circles of timber. Radiocarbon dates from its surrounding ditch show that it was built hundreds of years after Stonehenge. *See pages 10–11, 28, 45 46, and 63.*

THE RIVERSIDE PROJECT TEAM

Many experts and hundreds of volunteers have assisted Mike and the Riverside Project over the years. Here is the team's core group.

Josh Pollard is an expert on the nearby stone circle at Avebury and teaches archaeology at Bristol University. He joined the project in 2004, bringing many years of experience as a field archaeologist and Neolithic expert.

Colin Richards is an expert in Neolithic houses and stone circles who teaches archaeology at Manchester University; he and Mike have dug together for many years, from the islands of Orkney in the 1980s to Easter Island.

Julian Thomas is a colleague of Colin's at Manchester University; he and Colin have researched Durrington Walls for over 20 years, so joining the project in 2004 was the opportunity of a lifetime to gather new evidence.

Chris Tilley teaches the study of material culture at University College London. He is an expert on interpreting the landscape around monuments and joined the project in 2004. Many years before, he and Mike were research students together.

Kate Welham is an expert in survey and computing; before becoming a lecturer at Bournemouth University, she was a researcher in Mike's department at Sheffield University.

Paul Garwood teaches archaeology at Birmingham University where he is an expert in Early Bronze Age burial mounds. He joined the team in 2008.

Dave Robinson is an expert on the prehistoric rock art of California as well as the Neolithic period of Britain; he now teaches archaeology at the University of Central Lancashire. He joined the project in 2005.

THE EVER-CHANGING TIMELINE
OF STONEHENGE

I learned of Mike's work when the first stories about the Durrington houses were released to the world. Then I approached National Geographic, which is one of the sponsors of his work, about writing a book describing his discoveries. I began this process impressed with the Riverside team, thrilled to get to join them, and allied with one of their backers. I let you know this background because you should question the views in this book just as Mike questioned Atkinson's dates.

Shortly after I was last at Stonehenge, the archaeologists Timothy Darvill and Geoffrey Wainwright announced that they had solved Stonehenge—it was a center of healing, not a place of the dead. They had been given permission to dig at the stone circle itself and claimed they had new dates based on the evidence they had found there that supported their theory and challenged the Riverside Project's. You can find articles, photos, and blogs presenting their views on the Smithsonian website *(see* Online Resources, *page 64)*.

In June of 2009, Mike, Tim, and Geoff met and looked carefully at all of the available evidence that would help date Stonehenge. They agreed on the timeline you see on the facing page. Their conclusions are so new that the dating of the phases of Stonehenge you see here is different even from the sequence in the *National Geographic* article about Stonehenge. In fact, the scientific article they are writing together will only be published at the same time as this book. Mike also agrees with Tim and Geoff that in medieval times Stonehenge was associated with healing, though he and they still view the original use of the stone circle differently.

I urge you to read widely and not assume any one authority has it right. This book follows Mike and the Riverside team, but it is also just as much about an attitude of thinking and questioning that should be applied to all ideas, including those presented here.

TIMELINE

8000–7000 B.C. Hunter-gatherers on Salisbury Plain erected posts made of giant pine trees, close to where Stonehenge would be built 5,000 years later.

3800 B.C. Early farmers began to build tombs in the area. These were constructed of earth, wood, and stone and are called "long barrows."

3500 B.C. The Stonehenge Cursus was built at this time; it led to a long barrow at its east end *(see map on pages 10–11)*.

3000–2935 B.C. First stage: ditch, banks, and Aubrey Holes. The Aubrey Holes probably held bluestones brought from Wales. The holes were also used as burial places for cremations. Bluestonehenge probably built during this period.

2640–2480 B.C. Second stage: erection of sarsens at Stonehenge, with bluestones probably rearranged within them. Settlement of Durrington Walls surrounding Southern Circle (2515–2480 B.C.). Woodhenge may also have been built at this time or later.

2480–2280 B.C. Third stage: Stonehenge avenue's bank and ditch dug. Last cremation burials within Stonehenge. Bank and ditch constructed around Bluestonehenge.

2480–2460 B.C. Construction of bank and ditch of Durrington Walls henge enclosure on top of village.

2460–2280 B.C. Decay of the Southern Circle's timbers.

2300 B.C. The Amesbury Archer, an immigrant from Central Europe, was buried three miles from Stonehenge.

2270–2020 B.C. Fourth stage: bluestones rearranged as an inner oval in Stonehenge. Woodhenge's ditch dug.

2020–1740 B.C. Fifth stage: new circle of holes (called Z Holes) dug in a circle around Stonehenge.

1630–1520 B.C. Sixth Stage: new circle of holes (called Y Holes) dug in a circle around Stonehenge.

SUGGESTIONS FOR FURTHER READING

IN ORDER TO PREPARE for the book, I read all of the current accounts of Stonehenge available in books for general interest adult readers. In turn, these books describe earlier views of Stonehenge, from Geoffrey of Monmouth through William Stukeley and on to the present. Mike generously gave me several articles he has published, including the "Age of Stonehenge," where I found the Atkinson quote on page 32 of this book. I visited the team at Stonehenge in both 2007 and 2008 and interviewed them there.

While it does not have a category for Stonehenge or prehistoric Britain, the Archaeological Institute of America offers a list of books for younger readers interested in learning about ancient times: http://www.archaeological.org/pdfs/education/biblios/AIAkids_books.pdf; it also offers a page of lesson plans and activities aimed at teachers: http://www.archaeological.org/webinfo.php?page=10414.

NONFICTION FOR TEACHERS, PARENTS, AND OTHER ADULTS

Burl, Aubrey. *Stonehenge: A New History of the World's Greatest Stone Circle.* Constable, 2006.

Chippindale, Christopher. *Stonehenge Complete. 3d ed.* Thames & Hudson, 2004.

Darvill, Timothy. *Stonehenge: The Biography of a Landscape.* Tempus, 2005.

Larsson, Mats and Mike Parker Pearson, eds. *From Stonehenge to the Baltic: Living with Cultural Diversity in the Third Millennium B.C.* British Archaeological Reports, International Series, 2007.

Parker Pearson, Mike. *Bronze Age Britain. 2d ed.* Batsford, 2005.

Pitts, Mike. *Hengeworld.* Arrow, 2001.

Richards, Julian. *Stonehenge: The Story So Far.* English Heritage, 2007.

NONFICTION FOR YOUNG READERS

Many nonfiction series publishers have volumes on Stonehenge—some place greater emphasis on the unsolved mystery and others on the science of archaeology. Two books in series with a focus on archaeology are

Gray, Leon. *Solving the Mysteries of Stonehenge.* Marshall Cavendish, 2009.
Part of the *Digging into History* series, this recent book outlines conflicting theories about the stones.

Malone, Caroline and Nancy Stone Bernard. *Stonehenge.* Oxford University Press, 2002.
This book from the *Digging for the Past* series pairs an expert with a science writer and so offers more detailed information for middle graders.

And for a fun way to get a basic introduction to the site and its history, check out this popup book by an expert on Stonehenge:

Richards, Julian. *The Amazing Pop-up Stonehenge.* English Heritage, 2005.

ONLINE RESOURCES

The University of Sheffield in the United Kingdom hosts a site about the work of the Riverside Project at http://www.shef.ac.uk/archaeology/research/stonehenge.

English Heritage has gathered many resources related to Stonehenge and other sites of historical interest in the United Kingdom at http://www.pastscape.org.uk.

National Geographic offers its cover article on Stonehenge along with classroom resources at http://ngm.nationalgeographic.com/2008/06/stonehenge/alexander-text.

Smithsonian's different take on Stonehenge is available at http://www.smithsonianmag.com/science-nature/stonehenge.html.